With Love, from Trin.

Trinity Poasa-Uta'i

BookLeaf Publishing

India | USA | UK

Presentation by *BookLeaf Publishing*

Web: www.bookleafpub.com

E-mail: info@bookleafpub.com

ISBN: 9789357446129

First edition 2022

DEDICATION

Dedicated to the village that surrounds me, supports me and loves me.

But most of all, I dedicate this to my parents, Angela and Mack.

The people who have been there from day one and who continue to support me in my pursuit of self-discovery and success.

Thank you for being my inspiration, and two of my many muses in this life.

This is for you.

I love you, forever and always x

ACKNOWLEDGEMENT

THANKFUL | GRATEFUL | BLESSED

Firstly, I would like to thank the Heavenly Father for blessing me with the gift to write, and for blessing me with an opportunity to share this gift with you all, whoever may be reading this. I am thankful to come from a family of strong faith because this allowed me to build my relationship with You from an early age. This is all by the Grace of God! Beyond blessed.

To my real day-ones. My parents, Angela and Mack.
My best friends, my mum and dad. Parents usually say thank you to their kids for choosing them, but today I say thank you for choosing me! There really is no Trinity without you guys, and it shows. I love you both to the moon and back, and I am so proud to be your daughter. Everything I am and everything I do, I owe it all to you!

And finally, I'd like to thank my village for the constant support and the unconditional love you have all shown me. To those who have been here since day 1, and those who have joined along the way, to those who are related by blood and those who have become family beyond blood relations: I am extremely grateful for you all! Thank you for teaching, mentoring, guiding and loving me the way you do. There's no village like mine, and that's on period!

It's all love, always!

PREFACE

The poems in this book are inspired by Trin's
surroundings, whether she is in a room full of
family, friends and loved ones or when she is
alone and accompanied by her thoughts. This
compilation of poems describes how Trin sees
her life, and has allowed her to pause and reflect
on moments and memories that she is truly
grateful for. It has allowed her to reminisce
about her past, and acknowledge the people that
have been with her on this crazy rollercoaster of
life - those who have been there since day one,
and those who have joined her along the way.
Her family and friends - her village.

If you asked Trin what her biggest inspiration is
in life, she would say it is her village. The
people who she surrounds herself with in every
moment. But most of all, she is inspired bythe
people who were the first members of said
village. Her parents. Grandparents. Siblings.
Aunties. Uncles. Cousins. Extended family
members. The village that has supported her
since she was a young girl in Auckland, New
Zealand, right up to present day 2021, where
she's living her best life in sunny Brisbane,
Australia. In saying this, Trin also wouldn't be

who she is if it wasn't for her ancestors. Those who have gone before her, the generations of strong Samoan people who paved the way for her to have what she has and to do what she does. Big ups to all of the people in my life, this one's for you guys.

Another form of inspiration in Trin's life is her faith, and her ever growing relationship with our Heavenly Father. Although she has experienced a lot on her walk with God, and like others, has experienced doubt and strayed away from God, her journey has been strong and unwavering since then. She experienced temptations of worldly pleasures, and a constant wonder of things outside of the Church and her faith, but is a woman of God and a woman of faith through and through. In saying this, over the past year, she has grown and developed a lot in her faith, and has rebuilt her relationship with God, stronger than it has ever been before.
So, in true form, we will share one of her favourite scriptures, which comes from the first letter to Peter:

((1 Peter 4:10))

"Like good stewards of the manifold grace of
God, serve one another with whatever gift each
of you has received."
How Trin translates this is to do what makes you
happy. Do what fulfills you. Do the things that
you think you can only dream about. Live your
best life, and fill it with nothing but the best. The
best memories, the best company, the best
adventures, the best music, the best moments.
Thrive to make the best use of the time you have
on Earth.
This biblical passage is one of Trin's favourites,
and she hopes that it touches your heart like it
did hers.

Sending so many blessings and all my love to
you.
May these poems make you feel deeply, love
intensely and stroll down memory lane with
Trin.

'oute alofa ia te oe i taimi uma, fa'afetai tele
lava.'
Thank you, I love you so much.

blessings in
abundance.

Surrounded by grace and love
in the form of friends and family.
Generations past and present,
legacies of pride and love passed down over
time.
The lessons learnt at a young age
taught to me by my village,
I hold close to my heart each day.
Wear your name with pride,
be the person that God meant you to be.
Live life to the fullest, don't forget to pray.
Thank God in all instances,
and never ever forget your roots.
Love always, be loyal and true in all you do.
But the most important lesson of all

was to live a life worth remembering,
and to leave this place with memories,
not dreams, 'what-if's' and 'maybe's'
All glory to our Heavenly Father,
all my love to the village who gave me
everything I have,

All my gratitude, thanks and appreciation
To my village for these blessings I receive in
abundance.

|| John 13:34-35

Samoa: O Lo'u Fale

To the motherland,
To the birthplace of my ancestors.
and the land that I have only touched once
before.
To the home of my people,,
To our beautiful Samoa.
It has been too long
since I have touched your shores
and returned home to you.
But when I think of you, I picture
glistening waves in the clear blue sea,
thewarm and bright sun shining down,
the trees dancing in the island breeze
that carries the way of life in our islands.
The Cradle of Polynesia,
and the kingdom of my lineage.
To our islands & our home.
To Samoa - I love you
and await the time I will return
and feel at home once again.
But until then,
I will continue to learn about you.
I will dance alongside my Samoan brothers and
sisters,
Showcasing our culture with grace and love.

I will listen to the stories
Passed down through the generations
Of my Poasa-Uta'i family.
I will carry on the legacies
Left behind by our ancestors
And teach the next generations of
The strength, pride and wonder of our Samoan
culture.
Because I am Trinity Poasa-Uta'i
And Samoa is and always will be
My Home - Lo'u Fale.

my day ones

i will never know what it's like to be in your
shoes
or what it feels like to be a parent
but i am forever thankful
that God blessed me with you two.
This one is for the people
who I will forever rely on to get me through the
day,
the people i go to for anything and everything
and the people who have sacrificed so much for
us.
The people who have worked endlessly
to give us everything they didn't have growing
up,
And the people who have shown us the true
depiction
of boundless love in human form.
The people who have shown us that
they are all we will ever need in this lifetime.
To our best friends,
and the creators of our family.
To the people whose love story started this
whole thing
Back in 1998.
To our best friends,

Our day-ones,
And the people who we love beyond all human
comprehension.
To Angela and Mack
Thank you.
For all that you are, and all that you do.
For your love and your hearts.
For the love that brought you together
To create our family.
There will never be enough words
to truly describe how thankful we are
and how much we love you.
our only wish in this life
is to make you proud
in everything we do.
It's us against the world, always.
FAB5 forever.
kisses and hugs,
nini, nona and popi
(and koda & koco)

|| Ephesians 6:1-3

GOD > ALL

lifting all praise and glory
to the God who has guided me here
and has blessed me with all that i have
in this life of mine.
a woman of faith since very young,
and a forever-growing relationship with Him,
but i must say it has not always been easy
or consistent on my end.
I have strayed away from Him
and ignored His calls before
like the Prodigal Son we read about
in Scripture,
giving myself to the worldly pleasures of life
found in places other than in Him.
but in the end,
His call was consistent,
And he never gave up on me.
I was able to find Him
and put my trust and my faith back into His
plans.
I too have struggled
to pray and read my Bible daily
and have instead scrolled mindlessly
on social media to get my "church fix."
I have failed to attend church regularly

and haven't practiced my faith as much as I
should.
But I know He will always lead me Home
and I know my faith goes beyond the four walls
of a church or holy place
as long as I am consistent
in learning and growing
as a God-fearing woman of faith.
At times, I also feel as if His plans
are taking too long for me on Earth,
and that my timing in this life
is better than what He has planned.
But I know He will give me
exactly what I will need in the right time.

For His plans are better than my own,
His timing is greater than mine
and His grace will guide me to greater places.
All glory and praise to the Lord
for He is so good to me
and has given me so much
to be grateful for in this life.
So, to Our Heavenly Father I say
I thank You,
I love You, always.
Without You, none of this is possible.

|| Jeremiah 29:11.

kisses to the skies

If I woke up tomorrow
and saw you again
my heart would be full.
If Heaven had a phone
that I could call everyday,
I would be happier than ever.
To our angels in Heaven,
our brightly shining stars.
We miss you more than anything,
but know you are never too far.
And though we can't see you,
We know you'll always live vicariously through
us.
We know you are always with us
In our hearts and minds always.
Until we meet again,
But for now, sending kisses to the skies.

Alofa Ia Te Oe, Ia Manuia Lou Malaga.

|| Mormon 7:7 (The Book of Mormon)

practicing gratitude

something my parents and family always told
me
was to always practice gratitude.
to thank God for everything I have,
and the people who have gotten me to this place
in life.

i'm grateful for my family, friends, loved ones -
my village.
i'm grateful for my faith.
i'm grateful for good health.
i'm grateful for access to the basic necessities in
life.
i'm grateful for my Samoan heritage.
i'm grateful to have been born and raised in
Auckland, NZ and Brisbane, Australia.
i'm grateful for the endless opportunities granted
to me in this life.
i'm grateful for the gift to write.
i'm grateful for a stable job in times like this.
i'm grateful for the gift of world travel - and for
the experiences I have had so far in life.
i'm grateful for other cultures and ethnicities,
showing the richness of the human experience in
the world.

i'm grateful to be safe in all aspects of life.
but most of all, i'm grateful to be Trinity Iulia
Toaiva Poasa Uta'i, and for the life that I lead.

this one is for all of the people
who have supported, loved and guided me
on this crazy rollercoaster of life.
thank you for being you,
and for being on this ride with me.
i appreciate your love,
your light and your heart.

sousaday!

Tuk-tuks zooming up the dirt roads,
restaurants filled with strong scents of
Cambodian delicacies.
slowly driving through the arched gates as we
arrive.
Greeted by the happy faces of our students,
some playing futsal or having dance battles,
others singing songs or playing with their toys.
The outpour of happiness and love is insane,
smiles light up the entire courtyard.
Teachers roaming around handing out lunch,
students taking bread rolls and cups of water.
Students yelling "Teacher, Teacher"
Accompanied by their laughter and joy.

They have so little,
yet still smile and live with joy.
If someone can have so much love
with so little in life,
then I will live my life with a purpose.
To love wholeheartedly,
and dream as big as our students
at the Feeding Dreams school in Cambodia.
Thank you Cambodia
for giving me hope again

and inspiring me
to dream big,
love always and
practice gratitude.

#helpout2017

FAB5: est. 1998

My heart in true form
My family and best friends
it's us against the world

I love you always,
and hope that I make you proud
The loves of my life.

To my real day ones,
and my best friends forever
This one is for you.

the girl in the
golden dress

throwback to the 26th of march '21,
one of the biggest nights of her life
and the most fun she has had
in a very long time.
due to COVID, not everyone could be here
but thanks to technology and Zoom,
Family and friends from overseas joined
virtually from their homes.
the birthday girl, now twenty-one
strutting down the hallways
in a glittery golden dress
with makeup on and her hair did,
definitely out of her comfort zone.
surrounded by all of the people she loves,
her family, friends - her village.
old friends and family members
she hadn't seen in ages.
a true sight to be seen,
the room filled with smiles and laughter,
it was truly a night to remember.
big letters lit up in green,
which spelt out her name 'TRIN'

roses in glass domes like Beauty and the Beast,
such beautiful decorations for the tabletops.
a globe as her guestbook,
now filled with names and pictures
of those who came to celebrate this milestone.
her cake and 21st key
With designs inspired by the traditional Samoan
Tu'iga
as a celebration of her culture
and the beautiful Samoan woman she is.
her heart is so full of love
to all of the people who came out to celebrate,
in person and virtually,
And to everyone who sent their love and
couldn't be there.
special thank you to her parents
best friends and her nana
on all of their efforts
leading up to the big party.
it was truly a night to remember
and one of the best nights of her life.
cheers to twenty-one!
filled with excitement to see
what this new chapter has in store for Trin.
with a heart full of love
and so much gratitude,
to you from me - the girl in the golden dress.

season of waiting

accepting that this season i'm in
is the season of... well, waiting.
a time to practice patience
and accept that my time will come soon.
a time to pray and trust in
the plans that God has for me.
so until the day He will make His plans known,
I will prepare myself and be open
to all of His blessings and callings for my life.
And when He does bring something or someone
into my life,

it will all be in the right timing,
and I will be prepared and ready.

you do you

why do i care so much
about the thoughts of others
and compromise my soul
for the appreciation
and recognition of others.
So instead, I will tell myself:
just do you.
do not let others tell you
that you aren't enough
because you are everything
And so much more.
love yourself
and keep growing and flourishing.

rewind | pause | fast forward

gone are the days
of watching hi-5 and bumble on repeat,
when old disney movies were on a constant
rerun.
how i miss the days when mum and dad
would film our every move with the old camera.
when What Now! was the only thing on TV,
and my DVD collection was my favourite toy to
play with
when Mai FM would be the only thing we'd
listen to
and Nana's house in Mangere was the place to
be.

how I miss the days of the past,
That feels like over a lifetime ago.
 But here we are now
it's time to live in the moment,
be present in this life,

and cherish the memories we have.

switch off for a moment,
stop,look around and smell the roses,

and most of all, be present.
find joy in the small things,
spend as much time as you can with loved ones.

read, write, go out, explore
and don't stress about updating others
on your life and how you live it.
for someone once said,
right now, we live in times
where visibility seems to equal
to a successful and beautiful life.
so do not be afraid to disappear
for a moment, from everything
and see all of the things
that will be revealed to you
in the silence.
life is short, life is beautiful
but only when you choose
to be present and live to the fullest.

lowkey

a friendship like no other
bonds made strong over the time
that our love for one another
has grown and evolved.
for they are my chosen family
the people i call my best friends
wouldn't wanna do life with anyone else.
thankful always for my faves,
For their support, love and the endless laughs.
Here's to my favourite pack of hyenas
Chlo-money, Connor, Philly, Glo, Faith, Em,
Reeves, Mon & Courage (& Co.)
this one is for my besties.
lowkey, forever and always x

officially missing you.

I'm wishing on my shooting star
And I know you're never really far
away from here, from us, your home.
how everyday I wish heaven had a phone.
I wish I could hear the voices of our angels,
Just one more time here on Earth.
It has been way too long,
but I know it was their time to go.
To be with our Heavenly Father above,
and to rest peacefully, living on in our love.
So, for now, we can only await the day
when God will give us wings, and bring us home
with Him to stay.

something i miss: living out of a suitcase

living in the world
of COVID and lockdowns
has made the traveller in me
start to reminisce
about our previous ventures on an aeroplane
and where our big adventures took us.
back in '02, when i went to Samoa with Mum,
i can vaguely remember the whole trip
and live vicariously through the pictures we have
in mum's photo albums at home.
or in '07, one of our trips back to New Zealand -
i remember spending Christmas with the Uta'i family
Our last Christmas spent
with our Angel, Papa Uta'i.
or in '17, when it was the first flight i'd ever taken alone -
coming home from New Zealand
to go to a leadership conference

while the family stayed back
for our Noa-Aiono family reunion.
later on in '17, i hopped on another plane
and went to Cambodia with yLead -
experiencing the biggest culture shock
alongside such amazing and beautiful people
or in '19, when mum, the boys and I
ventured to Hong Kong and parts of Europe
on a family vacation (with dad travelling
virtually).
or the last time mum and i were on a plane
earlier in '21, on a flight back home to see Papa
Pili.
an emotional and long overdue trip
in the midst of these crazy times.
but not the last time
we will ever travel overseas.
for we are optimistic
that travel will return to normal & we can go
overseas again.

because to us, travel is the opportunity
to experience, learn and immerse ourselves in
rich new cultures.

So here's to life in a suitcase,
and to the hopes we can travel very soon.

pasifika and proud

thankful for the journey i've been on
where i have been learning and growing
as a Samoan woman in today's society
partaking in Siva classes with Tilomai
and mentoring alongside proud Pasifika peoples
at Mana Pasifika

I have learnt so much about myself
and my culture
in such a short window of time.
i give thanks to my parents and ancestors
who paved the way for us
as the next generations of Pasifika people
and for blessing us with our culture
which we carry with us in every place we go.

'faafetai mo la'u aganuu samoa, ma o matou aiga
ua mavae, taimi nei, ma le lumanai'
(thankful for my Samoan culture,
and for our families
past, present and future)

not our time, not our place.

not the right time,
and never the right place
it seems like we fit
but maybe this is just a facade.
two different puzzle pieces,
under the impression they fit together,
only to find out later
that they belong to two different puzzles
altogether.
that is you and i,
we fit together, but don't belong,
but holding on to something
that doesn't exist in this lifetime.
so, i guess this is it for us,
But it's been such a wild ride.

i will always have so much love for you,
but have come to realize you're not mine.
I'll always be here if you need, and I'll always
support you from a distance.
The boy who stole my heart a long time ago,
And the one I call my first love.

an embrace, only from the right person.

Who knew a hug could really be so much more?
Who knew an embrace with the right person
would feel like this?
Who knew it was his embrace I've been longing
for all this time?
Who knew it was him?
All this time, it was him.

An embrace as warm as the sun,
an empty hole in their heart, finally filled.
Two "friends" hugging physically,
but so much more left unspoken.

An embrace they both longed for,
but only one from the other person.

poetry in motion.

stepping out onto the court again,
I feel like there is still a part of me that lives
here.
memories engraved in the paint on the court.
flashbacks flow in my head of
What feels like another lifetime.

stepping on the court, ball under my arm,
brightly coloured green and purple uniform,
and the latest Kobe's on my feet.
square up to the ring,
jump, swish and flick.
hand in the cookie jar.
true poetry in motion.
how crazy to think that was my whole life at one
point,
training every day, playing every saturday.
been a long time since i hung up my boots,
but the memories i will always cherish
and remember fondly.

make her proud

13 year old me,
looking in the mirror.
stressing about big decisions
and what her future looks like.
fast forward 9 years, here we are.

make her proud.
make your family proud.
you got this!
don't give up.
remember your 'why'
and keep your head up.
if life knocks you down,
practice resilience.
if you get stressed,
practice patience.
if you get emotional,
practice self-control.
and if you ever fail,
know that it is better to constantly fail
than to give up and never try again.

luckily enough

luckily enough
the story is far from over.

don't give up
don't give in
pen in your hand,
paper in front of you.
the exciting part is only starting now
just take your pen and
write your masterpiece, sis.

luckily enough,
your story is just beginning.